DAISY GIRL SCOUT
ACTIVITY BOOK

Girl Scouts of the USA
420 Fifth Avenue
New York, N.Y. 10018-2798

National President
Connie L. Matsui

National Executive Director
Marsha Johnson Evans

National Director, Membership and Program
Sharon Woods Hussey

Director, Program Development
Harriet S. Mosatche, Ph.D.

Project Directors
Harriet S. Mosatche, Ph.D.
Trina V. Brooks

Authors
Trina V. Brooks
Sheila K. Lewis

Director, Publishing
Suzanna Penn

Senior Editor
Susan Eno

Designer
Kaeser and Wilson Design Ltd.

Illustrators
Christine Benjamin, pp. 35, 40-41; Randall Enos, pp. 3, 4, 9, 20, 21, 22, 24, 36, 37;
Eveline Feldmann Allred, pp. 12, 34; Christine Staehelin, p. 23; Liz Wheaton, pp. 5, 18.

Inquiries related to the *Daisy Girl Scout Activity Book*
should be directed to Membership and Program,
Girl Scouts of the USA, 420 Fifth Avenue, New York,
N.Y. 10018-2798.

© 2000 by Girl Scouts of the United States of America,
420 Fifth Avenue, New York, N.Y. 10018-2798

First Impression 2000
Printed in the United States of America
ISBN 0-88441-606-2
10 9 8 7 6 5 4

Who am I?
I am a Daisy Girl Scout!

My name is:

My birthday is:

These are a few of my favorite things:

colors   foods

hobbies   songs

stories

3

Here is a design of *my name* and *my favorite things* all rolled into one:

A Paper Portrait

This is my hair.

This is my face.

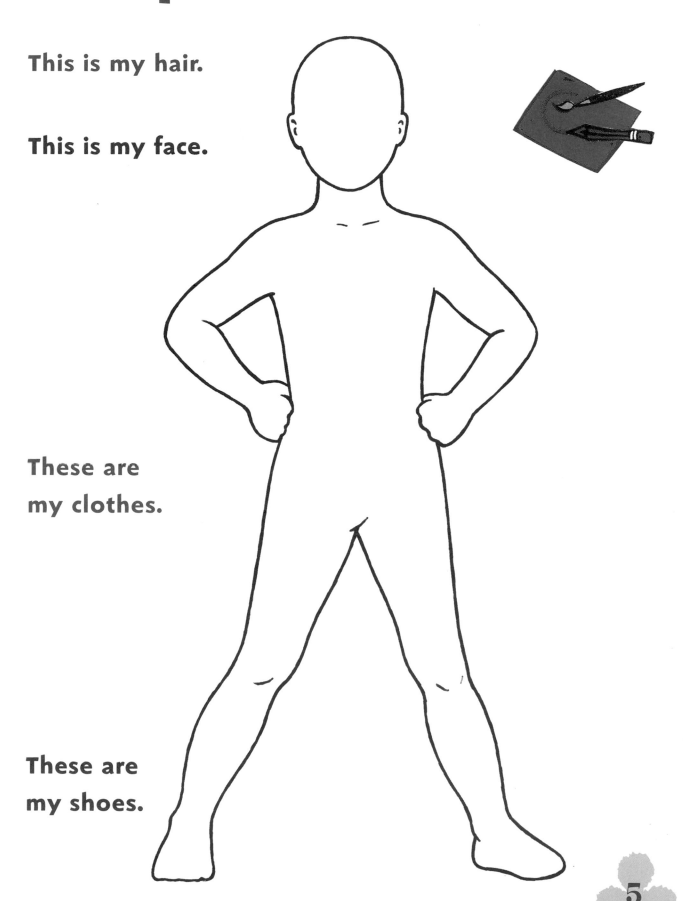

**These are
my clothes.**

**These are
my shoes.**

Daisy Girl Scouts Have Feelings, Thoughts, and Dreams

Inside my head, there are things you can't see.

My thoughts—My feelings—My dreams!

This is what they look like.

Thoughts

Feelings

Dreams

7

Daisy Girl Scouts Have Friends!

These are the names of my Girl Scout friends. (If you want to, you can have them write their own names.)

_____

_____

_____

_____

_____

_____

_____

The Girl Scout Promise

On my honor, I will try

To serve God and my country,

To help people at all times,

And to live by the Girl Scout Law.

Here is a picture of how I try to serve God:

And my country:

This is how I try to help people:

The Girl Scout Law

I will do my best to be

* honest and fair,

* friendly and helpful,

* considerate and caring,

* courageous and strong, and

* responsible for what I say and do,

and to

* respect myself and others,

* respect authority,

* use resources wisely,

* make the world a better place, and

* be a sister to every Girl Scout.

Circle your favorite line from the Girl
Scout Law. Draw a picture, or cut out
pictures from magazines, to show what
your favorite line means to you. Draw,
paste, or glue your picture right here.

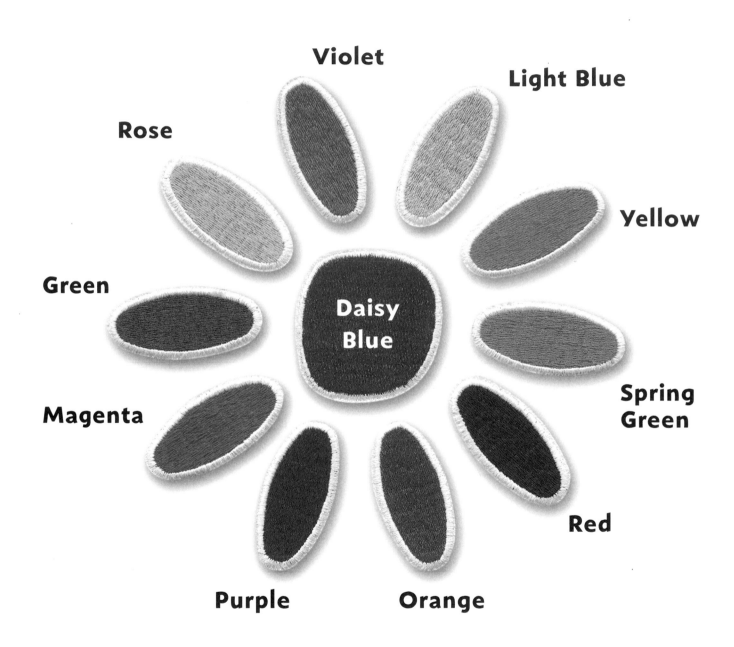

Violet

Light Blue

Rose

Yellow

Green

Daisy
Blue

Magenta

Spring
Green

Red

Purple

Orange

Learning Petals

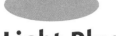

Light Blue
Honest and fair

Yellow
Friendly and helpful

Spring Green
Considerate and caring

Red
Courageous and strong

Orange
Responsible for what I
say and do

Purple
Respect myself and
others

Magenta
Respect authority

Green
Use resources wisely

Rose
Make the world a
better place

Violet
Be a sister to every
Girl Scout

Daisy Blue
(Promise Center)
The Girl Scout Promise

The First Daisy

The first Daisy (Juliette Gordon Low) liked to do many things.

- **She wore a watch that didn't work.**
- **She liked to fish.**
- **She had a pet rabbit.**

Draw one of them:

How are you like the first Daisy?

The Girl Scout Birthday is:

This is what we do on that day:

17

Daisy Girl Scouts

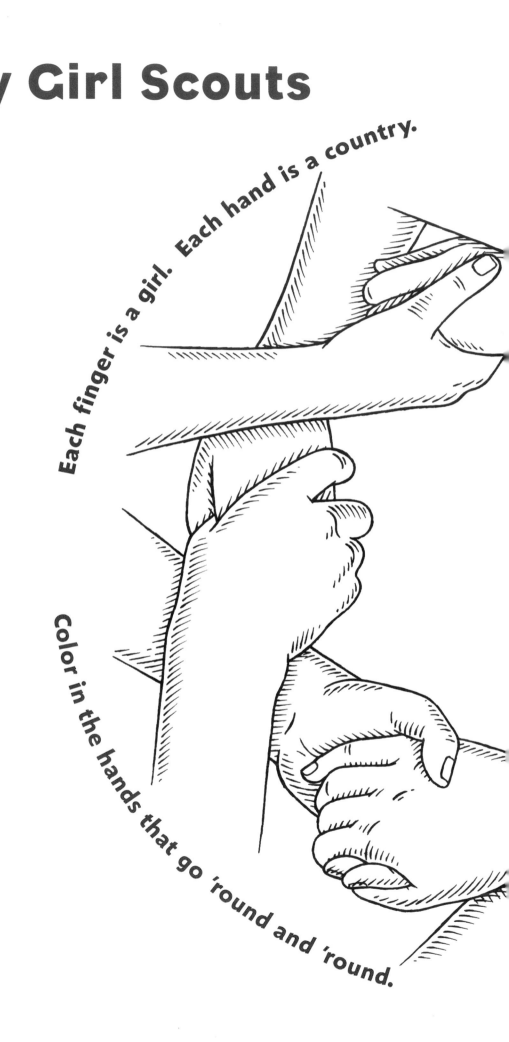

Each finger is a girl. Each hand is a country.

Color in the hands that go 'round and 'round.

18

Go 'Round the World

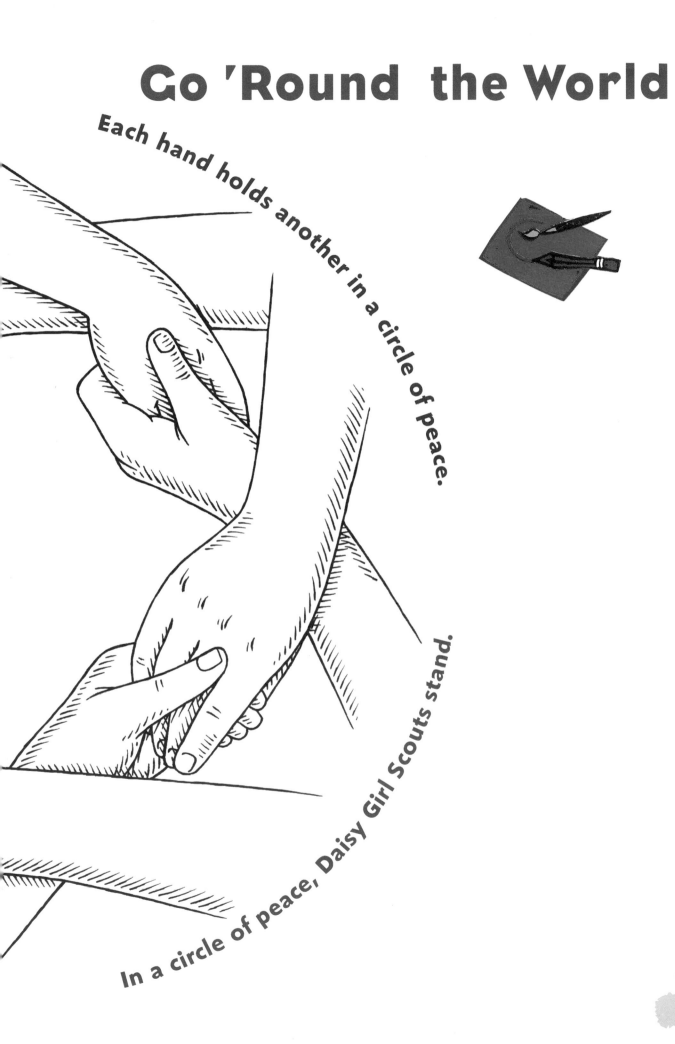

Each hand holds another in a circle of peace.

In a circle of peace, Daisy Girl Scouts stand.

19

Everybody Is Special

People are different.

Some people are tall.

Some people are short.

Some people like summertime.

Some people like winter much more.

Some people like to play sports.

Some people like to draw.

Some people like to run.

Some people use a wheelchair to go places.

No matter what they do, everybody is special.

Show how you are different from your friends.

Show what makes you special right here.

Alphabet Hike

Look around the room.

Do you see an object that
starts with the letter A? B? C?

Name as many objects as you can
that start with different letters of
the alphabet.

You can play this game outside, too.

Nature in Action

Nature is all around us.
Can you draw some things in nature?

What happens when the wind blows?

Where can you find sand?

What lights up during the day?

What shines in the night sky?

What happens to water when it's
icy cold outside?

What else do you notice about nature?

Cool Ways to Count

Here's a fun way to count to 10.

 Sing **1** song.

Name **2** friends.

Blink your eyes **3** times.

 Spin around **4** times.

 Collect **5** leaves.

26

Draw **6** smiling faces.

Clap **7** times.

March in place **8** times.

Look for **9** different colors.

Hold up **10** fingers.

You did it! You counted to **10**!

Discovery Boxes

If I had a shoebox,
I'd put my favorite things inside.
Like buttons, yarn, and pretty rocks;
Maybe crayons, jewelry, or lonely socks!

Draw what you would put in your shoebox.

Use Lines to Make Art

Draw a **squiggly** line.

Draw a **thick and furry** line.

Draw a **thin** line.

Draw a **curlicue** line.

Make a design using as many lines as you like.

Life Takes Shape

What kinds of shapes do you see every day? Can you draw them?

What shape is the moon? Does it change?

What shape is your front door?

What shape is an egg?

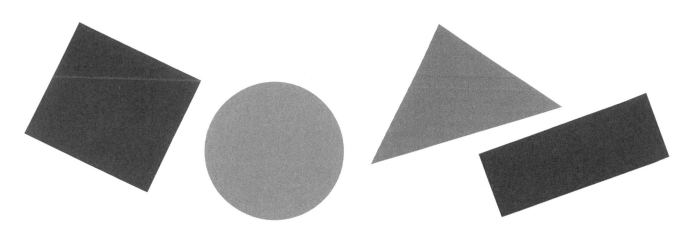

Can you make new shapes out of these shapes?
Give it a try.

Move with Me

I love to move, wiggle, and squiggle.

Which animal do you move like?
Color it.

Sometimes I like to be still.

What do you do when you want to be still?
Circle it.

I love to move, sway, and swish.

How do you move?
Circle it.

Sound Sense

Be silent for a moment.
What do you hear?

Do you hear a clock ticking?

Tick tock. Tick tock.

Do you hear a car horn?

Honk-honk. **Honk-**honk.

Close your eyes.

Do you hear more sounds?

Fewer sounds?

Open your eyes.

Can you see what you heard?

37

Popsicle Puppet

I have a lot of fun with my Popsicle Puppet.

Her name is _____ .

I paste her on a Popsicle stick

And she comes alive!

Look at her hair!

Look at her eyes!

Look at her face,

It lights up the place.

Let's put on a play with all of
our Popsicle Puppets.

Trace, decorate, and
paste to a Popsicle stick.

Popsicle Puppet Stage

My puppet needs a place to play.
I can build her a stage.
Here it is, with curtains and lights.

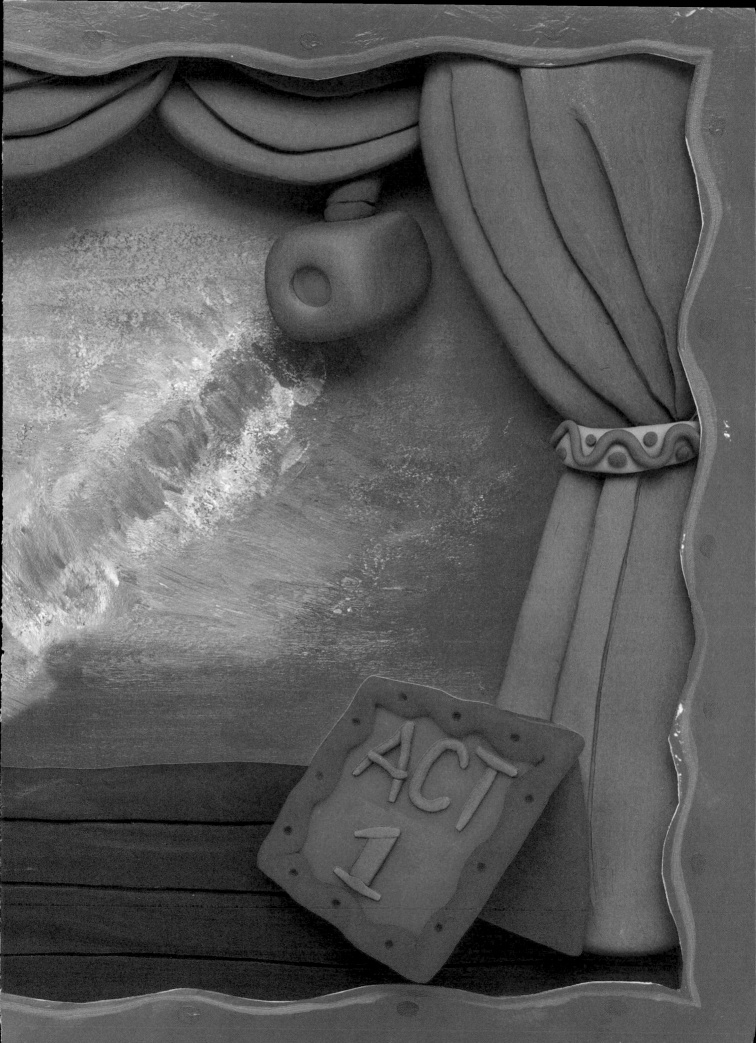

Meeting Melodies

This is the way I go to my Daisy Girl Scout troop, go to troop, go to troop.

This is the way I go to troop, and this is what I bring.

I bring my _____ cap,

I wear my _____ face.

I say hello and I take my place,

at my Daisy Girl Scout meeting.

Now that we're done greeting,

We can have some fun!

Fun is . . .

Fun is . . .

What other songs do you like to sing when you're with other Daisy Girl Scouts?

Can you sing a song right now?

At the end of your year as a Daisy Girl Scout, you can get ready to become a Brownie Girl Scout. What would you like to do as a Brownie Girl Scout?